the Heartbeat of a Greeter

A GUIDE TO THE
GUEST SERVICES MINISTRY

BY ANN CAMPBELL

The Heartbeat of a Greeter
A Guide to the Guest Services Ministry by Ann Campbell

Copyright © 2018 Ann Campbell. All rights reserved.

No part of this publication may be reproduced, distributed, or transmitted in any form or by any means, including photocopying, recording, or other electronic or mechanical methods, without the prior written permission of the publisher or author, except in the case of brief quotations embodied in critical reviews and certain other noncommercial uses permitted by copyright law.

Ann Campbell
acampbell@yournlt.com

ISBN-10: 0-692-98746-0
ISBN-13: 978-0-692-98746-9

Printed in the United States of America
Book Design: Kenyatta T. Harris
Editing: Dina - dinawrites.com
First Printing: January 2018

ACKNOWLEDGEMENTS

First and foremost, I give God all the glory, and I thank God for the heart that He has molded and placed in me. It has given me the opportunity to experience how a servant of Christ is able to love and reach those who enter into His gates.

I thank God for my Bishop, Daniel Davy, the man of God whom my mom would say 'I'm leaving you in good hands,' and the man of God that I can lovingly call Dad. Thank you for believing and trusting in me. You saw things in me that I did not know.

Minister Cyvonne Davy (Mom), oh how I love and appreciate you. I will never forget that Sunday morning on Fowler when you laid hands on me and prayed God's anointing to do His will. Your Words for me were to Pray and ask God for divine appointments. Mom, thank you so much because He's continually giving them to me.

My husband, Courtney, thank you for always encouraging and letting me know that I can do this and to always share this burden that the Lord has given to me for the lost. Your work behind the scenes will never be forgotten.

Pastor Collins thank you for always encouraging me and knowing how to find me when I'm at my lowest. Thank you also for always being there to remind me that God has called me.

Pastor Hughes you've always poured into me. "Sis Ann," you would say, "do not let it die." I'm doing it Pastor with the help of Sis Anne Dina Pierre (my Annemae), I hope it truly help someone.

Minister Dedric Scott, I can still hear you say, "Sis Ann you need to duplicate yourself." (Smile)

I Thank God for lending all of the following individuals to the Guest Services Ministry for a season to help build and shape this ministry into what it is today. You all have been so instrumental:

Julia White, Natasha Deodat, Katharina Wilson, Cheniqua Comer, Beth Taylor, Jamie Medina, Katrina Duenas

Carmen Richardson, my Faithful Sister, you helped this ministry so much behind the scenes with your follow-up phone calls, visitations with your sister until that last person on the list was visited.

The Mothers of New Life, thank you for teaching me the way of holiness. Mother Sonia Ferguson, thank you for always equipping and training me.

Mother Lucile Williams, you were my first teacher as a new convert and I will always appreciate how you taught and corrected me, thank you.

Mother Hattie Parker, I love and appreciate our daily talks.

I also want to thank those who have since gone on to glory. Mother Virginia Locke, I can remember you teaching me how to usher at funerals. "Follow me Sis Ann," you would say, and in my eagerness to learn, I would run behind you watching in amazement and taking it all in.

Mother Mary Davis, a true woman of God, I can still hear you say, "We have to be careful how we treat the people of God." I miss you so much!

Elder Willie Davis, thank you so much for allowing me to travel with you on those home and hospital visits. I've learned so much from those visitations.

SPECIAL THANKS

Thank you to the Ushers, Greeters, Benevolence Ministry, and New Convert Care team. I consider it an honor and a privilege to work alongside each of you. I LOVE YOU ALL.

TO THE LOVELY GREETERS...

My fellow faithful workers in the Kingdom, you share my passion and my burden in this dynamic ministry. Greeters, your role is like being a public relations agent for the church. What an awesome responsibility that is and I'm thrilled that each of you have embraced it. It's indeed an honor to work alongside such beautiful anointed ladies. God sees and knows the sacrifices that each of you have made to this ministry; the coming together, praying and crying to God before we can even touch the doors or the people, standing until your feet hurts (in those heels)... but yet you show up Sunday after Sunday ready to serve. Continue to smile, love, and reach for the harvest that God is sending us. You are all so unique, and God uses that uniqueness to showcase His love in the gift of helping. Remember to always face forward, open doors wide, and see them before they see you. And always remember to love with the love of Christ. My prayer is that God will continue to use you. May you remain steadfast so that you are able to stand to hear those glorious words: *Well done thou good and faithful servant, thou has been faithful over a few things, I will make thee ruler over many things. Enter thou into the Joy of the Lord. Matt. 25:21.*

Shannon Simon, Jaleesa Murphy, Diane Williams, Teeryka McLean, Ashley Mason, Temika Coker, Clay Osagie, Mother Joycelyn Carpenter, Alice Andrews, Ann Johnson, Angelina Colhouer, Kylia Campbell, Daniella Gordon, Kelecia Gordon,

Christy Konate, Caroline Adams, Roslyn Boodinsingh, Hernisha Reid, Toni Russell. Thank You!

To the dynamic Ushers…

You work hand in hand with the greeters. You all are always ready to serve and to lend a hand to that mother carrying a baby carrier, or to assist with a wheelchair. May we always remember we are servants of God and this ministry of helping is God ordained and God anointed. May your motto always be *"And whatsoever ye do, do it heartily, as to the Lord, and not unto man, knowing that of the Lord ye shall receive the reward of the inheritance for ye serve the Lord Christ."Col. 3:23-24*

Courtney Campbell, Kelvin Johnson, Kevin Story, Mark McLean, Derrick Thomas, Winston Powell, Mother Elsie Jones, Marvette Williams, Wilky & Patricia Saint Lot, Elder Eugene Gooding, Jose Adams. Thank You!

To the amazing Benevolence Team…

You all are a team handpicked by God. You work tirelessly behind the scenes, always giving of yourselves, your time, and your finances to make sure the needs of those that are in distress or grieving are met. The funerals, hospital visits, Sick and shut in, and the fundraising would not be a success without any of you. You are the heartbeat of the church, a Team that goes above and beyond to always fulfill the love of Christ. Matthew 25:35-40 King James Version (KJV) *35 For I was an hungerd, and ye gave me meat: I was thirsty, and ye gave me drink: I was a stranger, and ye took me in: 36 Naked, and ye clothed me: I was sick, and ye visited me: I was in prison, and ye came unto me.37 Then shall the righteous answer him, saying, Lord, when saw we thee an hungerd, and fed thee? Or thirsty, and gave thee drink? [38] When saw we thee a stranger, and took thee in? or naked, and clothed thee?[39] Or when saw we thee sick, or in prison, and came unto thee?[40] And the King shall answer and say unto them, Verily I say unto you, Inasmuch as ye have done it unto one of the least of these my brethren, ye have done it unto me.*

Alice Andrews, Lequita Williams, Candace Edwards, Mother Hattie Parker, Lisa Montgomery, Billie Williams, Janet Smiley, Valerie Richardson, Linda Lester, Tyrell Hamilton, Mamie Telfair, Mother Ceta Thorpe, Maureen Callum, Mother Joycelyn Carpenter, Angie Hebron, Caroline Adams, Rosslyn Boodinsingh, Desrene Wynter, Mark McLean, Kevin Diaz, Mother Elsie Jones, Mother Elsie Powell, Regina Campbell. Thank You!

New Convert Care

Pastor Samuel Pointer, thank you for your commitment to this ministry and your heart for souls. You sacrifice so much for the new converts, making sure they are well taken care of. Thank you for the encouragement and always taking the time to speak into my life. You're going to be missed.

To the ever patient Call Team...

As a part of Guest Services, you focus on building relationships with guest and new converts. This ministry is the initial point of personal contact that our visitors are exposed to. Thank You for making our guests and new converts feel special and welcomed through your follow up phone calls. The guests are given the opportunity to ask you questions regarding their experience at New Life, share their thoughts, and prayer request.

Carmen Richardson, Oneil Wright, Candace Edwards, Lauren Wilkerson, Akeem Stephenson, Ashley Mason, Kelvin Johnson, Clay Osagie. Thank You!

To the NLT Elite Team (Bus Ministry)...

Your role goes beyond a bus driver, each of you have built a relationship with the riders and it's so beautiful to see your interaction with each other. You're the first here on any given Sunday. You make sure that no one is ever missed. All of you love what you do and always ensure transportation is provided. You know each rider by name and that is amazing.

Tee Williams, Julius Brocks, Kevin Story, Mark McLean, Brandon Comer, Javed Morgan. Thank you!

Record Keeping - Baptistery

As in the Natural so in the Spiritual, Mothers (midwives) Ones who assist in or take a part in bringing forth; to bring about a result. You set the atmosphere and your job is just as important as any other because you reflect the rejoicing in the heavens as one soul comes to God. Patrece Lawrence, Kaitlyn Lawrence, Rhoshanda Pinson, Matthew Oneil, Alethea Richardson, Patrece Levy, Brandon Comer, Eldeen Morgan - you're the ones that make it happen in the Baptistery. You hold it all together, always prepared and ready to take care of the new born babes. It's much more than assisting in getting the candidates dress, collecting data, and taking pictures. You encourage and you nurture as in the natural so in the spiritual.

Reception Team

The environment in this room is very important. You welcome family members or friends to join the new converts in the reception.

Latoya Gatlin, Lydia Bennett, Jereme Jackson, Thank you!

Baby Dedication Photography Team

Thanks for your continued commitment to our Parents.

Del Rey Bonman, Latoya Gatlin, and Arlisha Myrie.

In Loving Memory of my mother Beryl A. Richardson and my aunt Elin Richardson, you both are the perfect example of sacrifice and giving of self. I love and miss you both so much!

PREFACE
Pastor Rashidi F. Collins

Passion is the one word that describes the evangelistic fervor of Ann Campbell. Passion undergirds her commitment to reaching lost souls with the life saving gospel of Jesus Christ. Her work ethic knows no boundaries with regards to outreach. She has literally allowed herself to become the embodiment of the Love of Christ as she ministers to those that walk through the doors of the church.

Sister Campbell invites guests into the presence of the Lord with warmth and sincerity and all our visitors can feel the genuine care that exudes from her. Much of her time is spent on the streets of Tampa visiting the thousands of people that come to New Life. In fact multiple souls have been saved as a result of her visitation endeavors and many are now productive citizens of the Kingdom of God due to her tireless efforts.

The passion that she personifies has been transmitted to the team that she leads. The sign of a good leader is the ability to reproduce in others the qualities that they possess. Those that work with her know that souls are the priority. Nothing is more important. Ever. As a consequence the level of intensity and excellence that her team brings to the table speaks to her ability to train, inspire and mentor others in the business of Evangelism and Retention.

It is of worth to note that the passion for souls that she presently exhibits did not start with her employment at New Life. As a member and as a volunteer she did her best to reach others with compassion especially those that were vulnerable and in need of extra attention. Many people have been blessed by the kindness that they experienced after interacting with Sister Campbell. She is a gifted, prayerful, God Anointed vessel that has come to the Kingdom for such a time as this. Her thoughts as presented in this book are the product of a lifestyle of passionate Evangelism. Embrace the Passion.

From My Bishop
Pastor Daniel M. Davy

"The Heartbeat of a Greeter: A Guide to the Guest Services Ministry" is a book to help any growing church build an effective Guest Services ministry. The chances of a first time guest returning to our church is enhanced when the first visit is enjoyable.. The guest service ministry is organized in such a way to make the visit pleasant and memorable and this should take place from the parking lot to the pews.

Ann Campbell draws on her many years of experience in our Guest Services ministry to offer some insights. The book is organized to facilitate easy usage of the material, pre-empt some common mistakes, and show how to establish a meaningful Guest Services ministry that enhances desired results.

This book will help all the major ministry leaders because in a real sense, we are all in the people business.

TABLE OF CONTENTS

Introduction

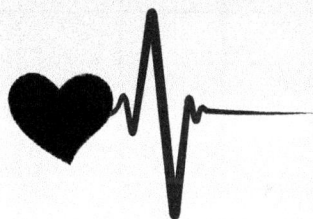

New Life Tabernacle, UPC was established in September 1992 to seek and save the lost in the Tampa Bay area. This ministry began at the University of South Florida, with a small congregation of approximately 20 members. Now, it is home to over 1,500 members, not including the membership of the nine churches that were birthed through this ministry.

What has caused this great level of success in membership? The answer is simple – showing the love of Christ. The love of Christ is what has always drawn people to Him. Helping others feel welcomed and comfortable has always shown positive results when converting our guests to members. Jesus says in John 12:32 And I, if I be lifted up from the earth, will draw all men unto me. The Guest Services ministry is designed to lift up Christ, simply by showing the love of Christ. By doing this, more people will be drawn to His church. And this should be done in the most effective way possible.

The Guest Services ministry provides a plethora of services, such as; ushers and greeters, retention, baby dedication, Bible study, hospital visitation, benevolence, and follow up. One of our main goals is to cater to the integral needs of those who attend services, by fostering a relationship between them and the church. Without appealing to the people attending services, whether they are members or visitors, there is no practical reason for them to return to the church. This valuable lesson is the driving force that has led me, the leader of the Guest Services ministry, to pen this book.

When I first stepped foot at the church I would forever call home, I was uncomfortable. I received an invitation from a niece whose baby would be dedicated to the Lord. I wasn't sure what to expect, but what I witnessed that morning made me uncomfortable. The people there were dancing, jumping, and outwardly praising God. This was foreign to me and so I thought there was something wrong with the church. That night, I went back to where I was more comfortable – the club. However, this time it was different. While there, it was as if I could see the pastor walking back and forth, on the dance floor, and for some reason, some of the words from his message came back to my remembrance. I ignored what I saw and heard and continued to live a reckless life.

It wasn't until October 26, 1997, nearly a year later, that I suddenly made the decision to stop going to the club.

That particular day, while at the club, the Lord began dealing with me. Then, as clear as day, the message from a year prior came back to my remembrance and the level of conviction I felt that day was so profound. Even with all of that, as much as I'd made a decision to no longer go to the club, I still wasn't fully sold on letting go of everything I knew and loved, for God, even the love of my life. I had previously scheduled a trip to Miami to celebrate a well-known event called The Carnival and I decided I wasn't going to miss it. En-route, however, I felt that something tragic would occur. You know how sometimes you just get a gut feeling that something bad is going to happened? I thought that I would be the one to die that day. The feeling I had was undeniable and it actually shook my very essence. Due to that reason alone, I decided to turn around. Not many days later, I received news that the man I loved at the time had died while overseas.

Devastation consumed me to the core. Thankfully, I had loved ones who did everything they could to encourage and comfort me. Several of them invited me to church, but I wasn't interested. I eventually called my sister, Carmen, and told her I wanted to go to church. She mentioned there was a Methodist church nearby. She made this suggestion because we were raised Methodist.

The moment my sister mentioned the Methodist church, I told her I wanted to go to that "little church" we visited the year prior. My sister asked why and I simply answered, "I don't know." It was years later that I realized that the Lord had his hand on me.

Carmen had learned that the church had moved, but was unaware of its new location. She was determined to find it, however, so she began her quest in locating New Life Tabernacle, UPC. Her persistency soon paid off and we attended the following service and have remained there ever since.

Note that as a member of the Guest Services team, determination and persistency is integral in the overall success of the ministry. We will discuss this further later.

When my sister and I first arrived, there was no fanfare. There were no greeters to greet us at the door and no one to even usher us to our seats. Despite this, there was something that just felt right in my spirit, like I was supposed to be there, and I felt welcomed. Although the church did not have all of the conventional elements of a Guest Services ministry, what they did have was the burden to connect with everyone who stepped foot in the House of God.

At first I was stubborn. When I would come to church, I would sit in the back. Many times, grief would take over and I would begin to cry. One of the mothers, Rosslyn Kennedy, would attempt to soothe and encourage me, but I would discourage it. I had a negative attitude because I simply wanted to be left alone. However, she refused to give up on me. She came to learn that I was from the Virgin Islands and used that to her advantage to connect with me since she lived there at one time. Her method became useful and I learned that in many cases, finding something in common with visitors increases the probability of transforming them from guests to members. This was also true with Julia Chance, who was a genuine woman, filled with integrity. We became close because she too was grieving the loss of a loved one. Our friendship blossomed and was integral in making me feel at home at the church.

My pastor was also a key factor in my decision to remain at the church. Not only did he deliver much needed messages through the preached word, he'd often follow up with me with a call. Those brief conversations were so important to me. Just to know that people genuinely cared for me made a difference!

After three months of attending services, I decided to be baptized in the precious name of Jesus. I was moved by a song sung by my pastor's sister. Tears began to flow down my face and I knew that it was time to finally adhere to the word of God, especially when pertaining to salvation. I went to the baptismal area ready to take a big step, then an incident occurred between me and another individual. I was so turned off by the attitude of that person that I opted not to get baptized. As I was leaving the baptismal area, Rosslyn Kennedy ran behind me and said, "this is nothing but the work of the enemy." You see, the devil attempted to spiritually abort me and had it not been for the intervention of the saints, he would've succeeded. This is why making a connection with your guests is crucial.

A few months later, Rosslyn approached me as I was going to leave the service in order to drop off my niece who needed to be home. Rosslyn stopped me and asked me a profound question, "Do you trust me?" She asked because she knew that I needed to be at the service, especially during altar call. She volunteered to take my niece home, so that I could enjoy the rest of the service. The result? I received the Holy Ghost that night! We must always remember that there is a war going on for their souls. This is why I often times go to our guests as they are leaving the services to encourage them to stay and receive what the Lord has in store for them.

I could have easily left that day and never returned. However, that would have caused me to be lost for eternity. It took observation, perseverance, and the willingness to be subjected to rejection from the saints to help me see what was at work that day. You must remember, in most cases when guests come through the doors of the church many of them are lost. They are not equipped to think in the spiritual realm because they are not of the spirit. That day, the only thing ready to rise up in me was flesh. That sister had an attitude so I was going to show her I was not the one. The enemy, however, did not win in what he'd set out to do because one of the saints was on standby for the Lord – watching. She scooped in and told my flesh to back down and my spirit man to come forth. I will forever be grateful to her, because had it not been for her allowing God to use her for my sake, I would have probably left that day and never returned.

In 1999, the church was preparing to host its first Ladies Conference. The Ladies Ministry leader at the time, Sonia Ferguson, suggested that I call the First Lady and see how I could be of service. I was known for being a decorator, so I naturally assumed that I would be asked to assist in that area. I was shocked when Lady Davy asked me to serve as a greeter. My initial reaction was "What?! She can't be serious! I don't know the first thing about greeting." However, I submitted, pushed flesh and doubt aside, and served in this capacity.

I had no experience or a true understanding of what this position would require, but welcoming people and connecting with them, even if it was for a moment, came naturally. This experience taught me that the only pre-requisite for this type of ministry is to be friendly and love people – the rest will be developed as you engulf yourself more in the ministry.

The Sunday following the conference, one of the brothers in the church approached me while service commenced. He'd informed me that the pastor wanted to know why I wasn't at the door greeting our guests. I was shocked and rudely replied that greeting was a onetime thing for me. And as soon as I said it, I felt convicted. I knew that I should be obedient and so I went to the door and served. People responded positively as they entered the building. It was obvious that having someone welcome them, connect with them, and show the love of God was making an immediate impact – not only for the guests, but also with myself. Because of my lack of experience as a greeter, I asked the Lord to teach me how to be effective in this capacity; I wanted to be used by God. Soon thereafter, Sister Davy prayed for me, confirming my call. And ever since, I've been blessed to connect with thousands of lives.

Growing up in a Methodist church in Anguilla was perhaps my first understanding of servanthood. This concept was engrained in my head at a very young age. As a child, I was involved in a girls' brigade, sort of like the Girl Scouts of America. Our motto was to "Seek, serve, and follow Christ." The lessons I learned from this program were not only ones of servanthood, but of selflessness. And this will be evident throughout this book.

The Heartbeat of a Greeter, serves as a guide in

23

building a dynamic and effective Guest Services ministry as well as developing methods to seek and to save the lost (Luke 19:10). If you want to see your church grow both in numbers and spiritually, then this book is for you. If you want to learn how to become more impactful through servanthood, then this book is for you. If you have a burden for souls then be sure to digest as much of the information found in the pages of this book, as possible. The mission is clear – Seek. Serve. And follow Christ.

Greeters & Ushers

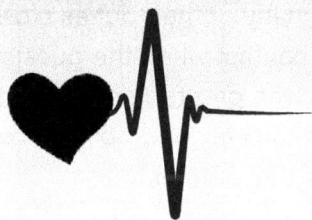

Understanding the roles of all involved in the Guests Services ministry is crucial for those who are in the various positions. Without a full understanding of the roles, it will be nearly impossible for anyone within the ministry to truly value their position and their impact on those they come in contact with.

The Guest Services ministry is a hospitality-based function within the church. Other than the physical setting of the church, those operating in this ministry help guests receive whatever the Lord has in store for them. This is especially true for those operating in the roles of Ushers and Greeters.

An Usher and Greeter exist to welcome the guests to their future home – the church. Simply put, these individuals make the guests feel welcomed. Although they serve in different capacities, many of their duties cross paths. Greeters are the first point of contact when the guests walk through the door. Once they've been greeted and served by the Greeter, the Usher steps in as their second point of contact. Let's first explore the duties of the Greeter.

With a simple greeting, guests instantly build a relationship with those they meet. This may seem farfetched; however, experience has proven that without greeting guests as they enter the service, it may discourage any further relationship with them and worst, may negatively affect how they receive the Word of God.

Like a hospitable hostess in a home, Greeters must be friendly, warm-hearted, and willing to accommodate the needs of the guest. It may be something as simple as giving directions to the restroom or Sunday school class. It doesn't matter; the guest must feel welcomed at all times. On the simplest level, Greeters are always representing something "special." In a church setting, they are representing their church, the pastor and leadership, and most importantly, God.

When people come into an unwelcoming environment, or they feel shunned by members of the church, they often associate that negative experience with God. This could lead the guest to feel discouraged in returning to the church, or any church at all - which is why it is vital to understand and respect the vulnerabilities that are encountered in the church setting. And with this in mind, the Greeter, along with other members of the Guest Services ministry must stay prayerful and humble in their efforts to be helpful servants, especially within the House of God.

In addition to being servants of God, a Greeter indirectly serves as a ministry of hope to the guest. I cannot count the number of guests who have walked through our church doors discouraged, spiritually broken, and unsure if what they need can be found in this House of Worship. By setting the tone and expectations for the guests, the Greeter provides a glimpse of hope to the guest.

I once read, "Mary worshipped at the feet of Jesus only after Martha welcomed Him in." This was a powerful passage to me. Can you imagine what would have happened if Martha would have had an attitude when Jesus came to visit? Do you think Mary would have been able to truly worship at the Master's feet if Martha hadn't set the atmosphere? It is vital that we understand that we cannot worship where the Master hasn't been received. Greeters set the atmosphere for worship. That alone is a POWERFUL calling. The roles of Greeters and Ushers are not one to be taken lightly. Prior to each service, the team walks through each pew to ensure that the area is cleaned and tithe envelopes are placed correctly in its slots. Boxes of tissues are strategically placed around the sanctuary and the altar area. The team also ensures that adequate bottles of water are placed on the platform for the praise team, moderator, pastors who sit on the platform, and the preacher. In addition, the team ensures that the bathrooms and baptistery areas are clean and prepared for the guests.

During the preparation of the building, it is crucial that the team remains prayerful. For instance, while placing the tithe envelopes behind each pew, the team prays over each seat. The focus is that the Lord would fill each seat with saints and those who are lost. While on the platform, members pray that the worship service and preached word would impact those who are in attendance and would cause a positive change in their life. More specifically, the team prays for those in need of salvation. Even when ensuring the restrooms are cleaned, the team worships. Once the building has been covered, the team ensures that the Greeters station is prepped with welcome packets, connection cards, and prayer request cards. Every area of the church has a designed purposed and although much of their work goes on behind the scenes, the Greeters and Ushers has a hand in almost every other ministry that takes place in the sanctuary. This ministry has a designed purpose! More on this will be discussed later.

Here are just a few tips when serving as a Greeter:
- Prayerful
- Focus
- Greet your guests with a smile and be sure to look into their eyes.
- Be intentional; look for ways to connect.
- Remember, first impressions are extremely important. If they form a negative impression of you, that impression determines how they'll view everything

else.

- Be sure to let the guests know you are available if they need anything.
- Greeter must be a soul winner; must have a passion for Christ and souls
- Can never greet with a rebellious spirit or with one's own agenda
- Must never greet with your back to the door.
- Must have a teachable spirit.
- Be excited
- Anticipate what your guests may need. A bowl of mints placed on the Greeters stations, pens and notepads for note taking, lotion placed in the restrooms. Think of what you would like or expect when attending a church service that would make them stand out...and then do it!
- Everything must be done with a spirit of Excellence! This may require the team to do a run through or practice the process or flow of welcoming. More on this in the next chapter.
- Remember God sent them and He will save them; therefore, greet with purpose.

The Ushers are the second point of contact. Once guests have been greeted, provided with pertinent information, and given a welcome packet, the Greeter directs the guests to an Usher.

Like Greeters, the Usher is also responsible for ensuring that guests feel welcome. Firstly, they greet the guests and direct them to their seats. Note that if the guest is carrying a car seat, the usher will offer to assist them with it. If the guest has a baby or a young child, the Usher will escort them to the nursery or Children's Church prior to escorting them to their seats.

Determining where to direct the guests is important. You want to be sure that they are strategically placed in a seat where they would have the best view of the platform. Because guests tend to be shy, placing them in the first few pews may intimidate them; however, avoid seating them in the back to eliminate distractions. You must also take into consideration the number and characteristics of the guests in each party. For instance, if someone within the group is in a wheelchair, it would be wise to find seating where the person in the wheelchair could be placed in the aisle while sitting next to their family member or friend. This may require the Usher to ask a regular church member to give up their seat. Again, the goal is to serve as a concierge to the guests; we want to provide them any support they need in order for them to feel comfortable.

In addition to directly serving our guests, Ushers serve as supplemental security. They ensure that all attendees are safe. The ushers handle these tasks by monitoring the restrooms and the various entrances. With a church as large as New Life Tabernacle, we understand that not everyone who walks through our doors have the best intentions; therefore, we must make sure that everyone is safe. During services, you may find Ushers roaming the Education Wing and Fellowship Hall areas making sure all doors are locked and secured to avoid entrance from those areas. The Ushers guide all attendees during offering and provide support to the Greeters, Pastors, and other ministry leaders when needed.

After Service
Reception

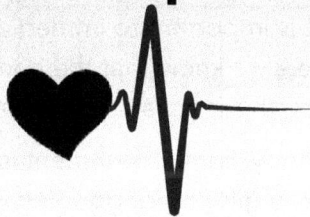

The Greeters and Ushers are important in setting the atmosphere for the service and ensuring guests feel welcome. But what happens after the service? The answer to this question is based on the guest's experiences. If the guest is baptized and/or received the gift of the Holy Ghost by the end of service, the guest is directed to a special Bible study. During the Bible study, we teach the *Proclaim the Truth* Bible study. This 20 minutes study, which was produced by the Apostolic Church of Tallahassee, is designed to explain the Salvation Plan according to Acts 2:38. Each new convert is given a fill-in-the-blank pamphlet, which allows the new converts to write down the salvation plan while the teacher is teaching. At the end, the convert is able to take the pamphlet home and digest the material. This is crucial, as the main goal is for the guests to have a full understanding of what they've experienced. Also, it is important to immediately remove any doubt they may have – we know that the enemy only wants to confuse new converts; this is a way to combat that.

After the Bible study, light refreshment is served and each convert receives a gift bag of goodies. This is another opportunity for the convert to connect with others. By now, you should have realized that connection is an integral part of the process. We not only want the guest to become a convert, we want them to stay!

If the guest did not convert, we invite them to come to a reception. At the reception, we serve light refreshment; get to know them a bit more. Experience has proven that it is beneficial to get to know the guest more, but be careful not to be too intrusive. An immediate benefit is that the connection "breaks the ice" and the guest would have identified someone in whom they can begin a relationship that is beyond the surface. By knowing a bit more about our guest, we are able to serve them more effectively and efficiently.

Also, in getting to know the guest, the Guest Service leader would be able to identify individuals who would be effective in following up with the guest and perhaps, serve as their Care Partner – more on this later. Because some information may be personal, it is crucial that all who are involved understand the need for confidentiality. There is nothing worse than a guest feeling betrayed. The lack of trust is detrimental to the possibility of their salvation. Ultimately, we are here to "seek and save the lost" and breaking confidentiality will ruin all prior efforts of reaching this goal.

The individual responsible for the reception should consider the following when preparing for the reception:

1. Time – This point is perhaps the most important of all. Although the service may be over, there is no knowing when the altar service will actually be over. There have been several services where dozens of people are being delivered, getting baptized and receiving the Holy Ghost. Should we wait until everyone is finished before the receptions begin? The answer is a resounding NO! We must consider the guests' desire to go home. For this reason, it is important to start the receptions as soon as the guests arrive. An exception can be made with those partaking of the Bible study; a rotation of lessons may be necessary.

2. Location – It would be best to host the reception(s) in separate rooms. If multiple rooms are not available, consider hosting the *Proclaim the Truth* Bible study on one side of the room, and the general reception on the other. Although this is not the preferred method, use this opportunity to invite the guest

to join the Bible study. Note that you may have to become creative in the "connection" process. For instance, form a team whose goal is to quickly connect with one guest. After the reception, host a brief meeting among the team to discuss what they've learned. It may be beneficial to write down the information and provide it to the Guest Services Director.

3. Décor – Be sure that the room is cleaned, and the ambiance is inviting. Consider placing table cloths on the tables and add a simple centerpiece. Personal touches lets the guests know that they are important. Consider investing in cloth tablecloths as opposed to plastic. Because receptions are held weekly, the investment would be worth it – financially. Although it is ok to display the same centerpieces every week, I would change it from time to time. However, always be mindful of your budget.

4. Refreshments – Because the receptions are short (no more than 30 minutes), keep the refreshments light. At New Life, we serve a dessert and a beverage. We want them to be refreshed, but the primary focus is salvation. Stay focused on what is important. Also,

5. Children – Our church have produced a coloring book for children – *Saved the Bible Way*. It is always good to have something to keep the children occupied while you are connecting with the parent/s. By providing each child a copy of the coloring book (with crayons) or some form of an activity, parents are able to remain focused on what you have to say. Be sure to consider children when planning the receptions.

6. Partnership – The involvement of other ministries in this endeavor is necessary. For instance, working with the Record-Keeping ministry (these are the individuals who assist guests with the baptism. They also maintain a record of each conversion). This team may be beneficial in escorting new converts to the Bible study. Greeters and Ushers can also assist in escorting guests.

Once the initial connection has been made, what happens next? This is what we will explore in the next chapter – Follow Up.

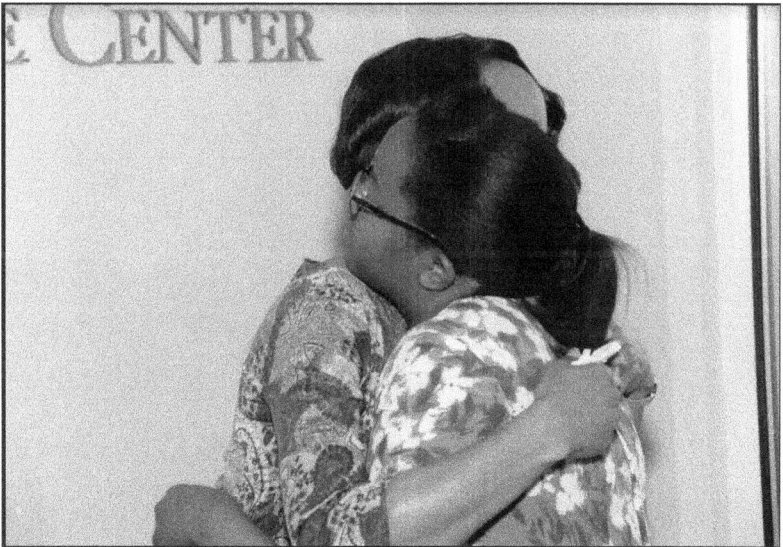

Follow Up

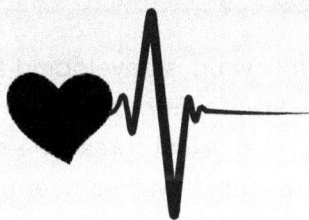

Follow Up is the next step to converting guests to new members. In this chapter, we will discuss four crucial steps when following up with visitors (and new converts): data entry, first time visitor follow up letter, follow-up calls, and visitations. But why is this important? Does it take this much work in order to retain visitors? Yes!

Church retention rate is highest when follow up is done within the first 48 hours. This is why it is important that the Follow-up team act quickly. From my experience, retention rates of first visitors is about 32%, second time visitors, is 50%, and third time visitors is about 75%.

Statistics shows that 85% of guests return if visited within 36 hours; 60% return if visited within 72 hours, and only 15% return if visited within 7 days. Anything beyond 7 days is not fruitful.

The first step in follow up is developing an effective database to input the visitor's information. In the beginning of our ministry, we used an excel spreadsheet to maintain the visitors' contact information; however, over time, this became ineffective, especially in times of searching for specific information regarding the visitor. For this reason, we searched for software that would be more conducive to the growth of our membership. Although there were several options to choose from, we eventually settled for *PowerChurch Plus.* This software has proven to be an essential tool for maintaining not only visitors' information, but also our new converts and members. We are able to schedule events, input their birth date, anniversary, the date of their baptism, etcetera. What I like most is the ability to send communications via email, phone, or the postal service. This is all managed in one software package. More importantly, it is user friendly! I cannot stress the importance of ensuring that the software is user friendly. As a leader, it should take you minimal efforts to train your team in this area.

Needless to say, with our database, we are able to reach as many guests as possible but what you do with the information is doubly important. This brings me to the next step in follow-up- the letter. The first time visitor follow up letter is personally signed by the pastor and mailed the day after the service of their visit. For our church, we mail letters on Mondays and Thursdays. These letters are designed to make our guests feel at home. It highlights services offered and ministries which they can become involved. Below is an example of our letter:

September 1, 2017

Mrs. Ann Campbell
6912 Williams Road
Seffner, FL 33584

Dear Mrs Campbell:

We are very excited that you visited our church recently. We hope you enjoyed the service and felt the warm welcome intended for you. You, as a visitor, added a special touch that would be lacking without you. Thank you for encouraging us with your presence.

We know that visiting a church for the first time can be awkward and overwhelming; however, here at New Life Tabernacle, we are confident that you will feel at home, meet many wonderful people, and know that you are loved and appreciated. Our pastoral and ministry staff is here to serve you and we would be honored if there is any way we can pray for or minister to you and your family.

There are several services that are immediately available to you. These include:

- Home Bible Studies
- Baby Dedications
- Marriage Classes and Counseling
- Food Bank
- Parenting Classes
- Leadership Training

For more information about our church, upcoming events, and services visit us at www.yournlt.com or call the office at 813.740.1868 where our ministerial staff will be available to answer your questions.

We look forward to seeing you again very soon.

Sincerely, because I care,

Rashidi F. Collins
Pastor

While our guests are awaiting their letter, the Call Team begins the third step of the follow up plan. That is, follow up calls. Again, an efficient database is essential to this process. Our team is able to generate a list of guests that must be contacted via phone. During the call, guests are thanked for attending our service. After, the caller allows the guests to detail their experience during the service. This helps us to know whether or not we were effective in making them feel welcomed as well as if the worship experience and the preached Word were impactful. If they were baptized and/or received the gift of the Holy Ghost, we ask that they detail their experience. We also ask if there any questions they have regarding their experience. Finally, we get to know them as an individual – are they married, do they have children, are they a student? Getting to know them beyond their initial experience at the church helps the guests understand that we care about them.

No matter the growth of our church, home visitations is a staple in the follow up process. There's something to be said regarding one-on-one interactions between the church and its guests. At New Life, we do our best to conduct visitations within one week on their visit. At times, this proves to be a challenge as we average 35 visitors per week. This is why calls are important, in the event you are unable to visit everyone. The Follow Up Team goes on visitations at least three days a week. That's right; we dedicate the entire day to visit our guests.

Much preparation goes into home visits. Firstly, a list is generated. Then a route is planned based on the addresses obtained. Thirdly, calls are made to the guests informing them of the visit. This is needed as some guests may have prior appointments or are employed, at which time the visit is conducted at their workplace – if permitted. Next, the team assembles gift bags for each guest – who doesn't like a gift? Each week, the gifts contain different items as most of the gifts are donated to the ministry. Some gifts include: Bibles, CD or DVD of the service the guest attended, journals, pens, books, flyers of upcoming events, snacks, lotion, and etcetera. Finally, the team, along with the ministerial staff, prays over the gifts and each guest who will be visited.

When conducting a home visit, be intentional during the visit. In other words, ask yourself, what do you want to accomplish? For us, the goal is not only to show our appreciation for their visit, but also to provide them with additional information about the church. We also encourage them to visit again, and if they have not had a bible study we do our best to schedule one for them. Our guests are grateful for the visitation and the chance of them visiting our church increases tremendously. Again, be intentional. My goal is conversion; home visits are simply a way to guide our guests in becoming new converts and eventually members. I cannot tell you the number of times visitors were baptized in Jesus' name due to a home visit.

Here's what two members had to say about their experience with the follow up team:

I am excited and honored to share some encouraging words about a woman of God, Ann Campbell. She visited my home over a year ago and that is how our friendship began. Not only did she visit me, periodically, she took time out of her busy schedule to call me and check to see how I was doing. Every time she contacted me, she offered some encouraging words of prayer and conversation. We usually found ourselves talking about scripture, family, church and how God has come into our lives and given us the opportunity to be a light for someone else. I do and always will embrace her friendship. I thank God for her faith and commitment to reaching people." - Angie G Clayter

What I have come to know about Ann are the following:

1. *Ann has a powerful love for our Lord Christ Jesus.*

2. *She is a powerful prayer warrior.*

3. *She has a powerful burden for wanting people to get baptized in Jesus name.*

4. *She never forgets a face or a name.*

5. *She puts herself last when it comes to helping others.*

6. *She is very sensitive to the feelings of others.*

7. *She is never too busy to help you have a better understanding of the Word.*

If my memory serves me correctly, I met Ann on Mother's Day 2015, because my granddaughter, Bonnetta, brought me and other family members to the church. Ann came up to us and introduced herself. She made us feel very welcome with her beautiful smile and the service was amazing. After service, Ann asked me if I wanted to get baptized. I didn't that day, but I told her I would come back to next week's service. I did, and she asked me again about getting baptized. I was not ready, but Ann didn't give up on me. So I was invited to have a Home Bible Study, which I agreed to.

The following week, Ann and Mother Hattie Parker came to my home at 10AM and conducted a Bible study. During that visit, I recall receiving a gift from the church, which included a writing tablet that I used to take notes. I also received a pamphlet titled "The Seven Steps of Salvation," which I have until this day! I was touched by the gift

Ann took her time and explained each step to me and my sister Brenda, whom was also at the Bible study. At the closure of the Bible study, Ann asked me again about getting baptized in Jesus name. How could I not after listening to her speak about our Lord Jesus Christ and what His salvation could do for me and what He had done for her in her life? I then knew I wanted this for my life. So she, along with Mother Parker took me to the church where one of the ministers baptized me in Jesus' name.

When I graduated from Home Bible Study, I thought she would just bring my certificate of completion or simply hand it over to me at church. I was shocked to see that my certificate was presented to me in front of the entire congregation! Not only was I presented with the certificate, Ann also gave me a lovely bouquet and a gift bag! I felt special.

I think about it now; Ann helped me to become a part of the body of Christ that day. I will always be thankful and grateful to the Lord for making her a part of my life. She became my first Sister-in-Christ. Through her continual follow-up, she encouraged me to attend two district ladies' conferences. The 2016 conference was amazing. The worship experience and the word were simply awesome. But the 2017 conference was powerful and amazing. During this conference, Ann wasn't feeling well, but she didn't allow her health to stop her from praising and worshiping God as well as allow herself to be used by God. At the conference, one of our Sisters-in-Christ was going through something. I saw Ann do what I believe is her gift. Ann got on her knees and began praying to the Lord for our sister. Ann interceded for her with everything in her, praising and crying out to the Lord to help our Sister-in-Christ. It looked to me that Ann was praying for a breakthrough and for her deliverance, and I saw how much Ann has faith in our Lord. But it didn't end there. When the service was over, Ann continued to pray and call out to the Lord for our sister and asked several of us to pray and worship too. She gathered us into a room where we worshiped, prayed, and read scriptures. I know our Lord was there because after awhile our sister seemed to be at peace. This was indeed a powerful experience and taught me the importance of intercession, unity, selflessness, and showed me the love of God in a unique way. - Sis. Maimie

Bible Study

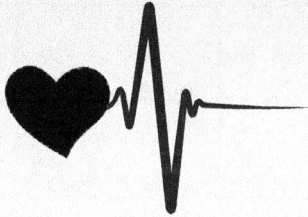

This chapter will be short; however, the content is extremely important when converting a guest to a member. When someone experiences God is a new way connection is important and one way to connect is via discipleship.

Apostle Paul tell is in Titus 2:4 that the older women in the church "...may teach the young women to be sober, to love their husbands, to love their children, to be discreet, chaste, keepers of at home, good, obedient to their own husbands, that the word of God be not blasphemed." In other words, they were to disciple.

Let's not forget Christ's commandment to his disciples in Matthew 28:19 & 20 – "Go ye therefore, and teach all nations, baptizing them in the name of the Father, and of the Son, and of the Holy Ghost: Teaching them to observe all things whatsoever I have commanded you: and, lo, I am with you always, even unto the end of the world. Amen." For this reason, Bible Study and a Care Partner program is encouraged.

At New Life, we offer several Bible studies; however, the premiere Bible study is called Exploring God's Word, which is available at the Pentecostal Publishing House. This study comprises of 12 lessons covering the entire Bible. Teachers can use the spiral bound chart or power point presentation that accompanies the lessons. There are also student sheets, which are helpful when the student study on their own. There are other studies such as, *Search for Truth*, which is also available at the Pentecostal Publishing House. Most of our membership has completed the Bible study and this is a testament that in order to grow your church, Bible study must be conducted.

As the word declares, *Two are better than one, because they have a good reward for their toil. For if they fall, one will lift up his fellow. But woe to him who is alone when he falls and has not another to lift him up! (Ecclesiastes 4:9–10).*

The Care Partner program is an accountability program that was implemented several years ago. We assign each new convert to a member of the church. The member must be willing to contact the new convert at least once a week. During their conversation, the member encourages the new convert, as well as assists them where they can. I should note that assistance is done on a limited basis to prevent our members from being taken advantage of. For instance, we do not encourage our members to provide financial support to the new converts; however, if the convert happens to be in need of food, the member will direct them to our food bank.

The Care Partner is encouraged to share scriptures, worship songs, sermons, books, and words of encouragement on a daily basis. I have found that not only are the new converts strengthened by the daily interaction, they are encouraged to invite others to share in this great experience. Also, the Care Partner reminds the new convert of any upcoming events and classes that may be impactful in their live. Weekly updates from the Care Partner must be submitted and they are to remain a partner until the new convert is fully absorbed into ministry.

Parking & Security

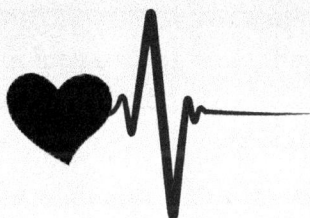

I'm sure that by now you know the Guest Services ministry is one that has many facets. It takes people that have a true desire to keep organization and order inside, and even outside of the church to limit distractions and to ensure that the Spirit of God is able to flow freely. One of those facets is Parking and Security. In order to ensure there is no chaos outside of your church, you want to make sure you have people in place to direct parking and ensure that people are able to get in and out of the church's parking lot without hindrances or accidents.

Completing this task, although simple, is quite imperative that it is done correctly and purposefully, strategically placing individuals in stations outside of the church just as you would inside. These individuals must have a willingness and a desire to work hard at all times. In many cases, especially if you're in Florida, the temperatures outdoors can be quite unbearable at times. You want to make sure your ministry workers are prepared and know to keep themselves hydrated.

Not only are the men required to direct traffic, but they also go even further. There are many rainy days during the hurricane season in Florida and one of their tasks is to park cars for members and guests who do not want to get wet before service. Again, remember, our main goal is to make sure that our members and guests are comfortable. We want to draw guests in and retain the members we have. We also assist by offering golf cart rides to guests who park too far from the church building and would like to ride to the main entrance.

Parking and Security positions overlap in the same sense that the greeters and ushers do. For instance, the parking attendees may also work hand and hand with the security staff to ensure that cars are safe while members and guests are worshipping inside. The church is meant to be a hospital, which means many people who are there visiting are sick, spiritually. Also, understand that the enemy is still roaming to and fro seeking whom he may devour. This means that not everyone that comes on church grounds come with good intentions so security is necessary.

The security team is also responsible for creating a safe environment for the parishioners. On many occasions, while service is in section, you will notice security walking around the church grounds making sure doors are secured and there is no suspicious activity going on inside or outside of the building.

Recently, I decided to try something different. I've discovered that on many occasions, thinking outside of the box or going against the grain has been beneficial and it is during these times that we find members and guests are most pleased. I wanted to do something that would bring a smile to the faces of our guests (and members) —something to brighten up their day. My First Lady came to me with a suggestion. She had recently attended a service out of state where their greeters held signs with phrases meant to welcome their guests. I thought this was a brilliant idea and would definitely be useful in achieving my goal. We purchased large signs with the following verbiage:

- Welcome
- You belong here
- You are awesome
- You look lovely
- You Matter

Members and guests alike have expressed how the signs brighten their day and make them feel loved, welcomed, and awesome. This confirms that the vision was executed in the way in which it was intended. Remember, what may seem simple is actually a lot when God is in it. One should always put forth their best effort when they are in ministry because even though you are representing yourself, your church, and your pastor, you are mainly representing Jesus and everything you do should ultimately be unto Him.

Going
Beyond

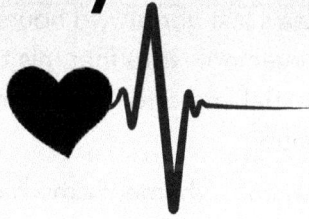

Developing a plan is crucial in retention! This can be achieved by connecting the guests (and new converts) to the ministry and individuals. For this reason, the Guest Services Ministry must be readily available to go beyond the basic duties of servanthood. There are several opportunities to connect and retain your guests:

RETENTION SOCIAL MINISTRY

Once a quarter, we host retention socials - one for women and the other for men. Separating the genders is not only more manageable, it also allows each group to bond in their own unique way as well as discuss topics that they'd probably not be willing to discuss in the presence of the opposite sex.

These socials last about two hours in length and are held on a Friday evening. Note that this time works for us; however, through trial and error, determine what works best for your congregation.

Each social has a theme. Some past themes include: spa night, BBQ show down, spiritual healing, and more! We have guest speakers who discuss various topics impacting our members. And we put much effort in the décor. Remember, doing this shows guests that they are special. I should note that several of our décor are recycled (i.e. linen tablecloths) or donated. Doing this does not break the bank and the funds can be better served elsewhere - like a building fund!

Finally, be sure to serve plenty of food!

NEW MEMBERS' CLASS

The New Members class is a program that is organized via our Education Department; however, the Guests Services team works closely with the Education Department as most of the attendees are guests. It is designed to help our new members, transferred saints, and new converts understand and become part of the vision of the church. Classes are held for four weeks.

Again, the Education Department is responsible for the overall operation of this course; however the Guests Services ministry ensures that communication is sent to the prospective attendees. This is done via mail and postal service. Here is a sample letter that is sent within two weeks prior to the class:

September 1, 2017

Mrs. Ann Campbell
6912 Williams Road
Seffner, FL 33584

Dear Mrs Campbell:

You are invited to attend New Life's New Members Classes on July 2nd, 16th, 23rd, and 30th. In these classes, you will be presented with the vision and mission of New Life Tabernacle, UPC. You will receive insight into our organization and will be informed of various ministries that you may consider becoming involved in. This is also a time for you to ask questions that you may have regarding New Life Tabernacle or other concerns. The classes will begin at 10:00am in the Fellowship Hall.

We look forward to seeing you there.

Sincerely,

Sis Ann Campbell
NCC Department Head

BENEVOLENCE MINISTRY

The purpose of the Benevolence Ministry is to serve those during their time of bereavement or crisis. It is important to see the love of Christ, especially during hard times. Traditionally, Benevolence Ministries provide financial support during their time of crisis; however, I believe that at times, more assistance is needed. For instance, assisting someone in cleaning their home after they've delivered their baby. At times, we assist others by taking them to their doctors appointment. I understand that it is impossible to serve everyone in this capacity; however, the point is to go beyond the minimal call of duties - their souls make depend on it.

FUNERALS

Believe it or not, funerals are a great opportunity to show the love of Christ. I cannot begin to tell you the number of times I've reconnected with a former guest or member at a funeral. As a result, several of them have returned to the church and are thriving spiritually. God has truly used these sad times to reach the lost and to heal the broken hearted - more on this later.

When a saint or a member of their family passes away, the Guest Services ministry steps in to assist the family. We are sure to be there from the beginning to the end. We assist the family in securing a location for the service, a funeral home, recommending a cemetery within their budget, order of the service, design and printing of the program, serving as greeters during the funeral, attending the wake, decorating and providing food at the reception, and more. This may seem like a lot, and it is! However, the reward is well worth it. Here is a powerful testimony from one of our members:

On February 11, 2017, my mother Milliane Pierre passed away after being ill for nearly two decades. My mother was such a fighter and had overcome so many health issues that her passing was beyond devastating. I did my best to pull myself together and simply celebrate the time I had with my mother, but doing so proved to be challenge. I know some thought it odd that I did not cry and engrossed myself into my work. I felt that I needed to be level headed, especially since I was tasked to spear head the planning of my mother's funeral.

I soon became overwhelmed with the planning and wondered how I would pull it off. I had not told anyone of how I felt; however, somehow, Ann and her team knew. Ann asked me the question I longed to hear - "How can we help?"

The Guest Services team volunteered to serve as greeters at the funeral, caterers during the reception, and a shoulder to lean on whenever I needed it. I was especially touched by their gesture since my mother was not a member of the church. I should also note that several members of the ministry would often visit my mother while she was in the hospital.

Their act of love during my time of sorrow was such a blessing in many ways. Firstly, it reassured to me the love of God. Secondly, their act of love and kindness was a great witnessing tool for my family. Several of my siblings came to church the following day and it was due to the impact that my church, via this ministry, made at the funeral. Thirdly, this served as a reminder of how we ought to treat and serve one another.

I will be forever grateful to my church, especially the Guest Services ministry. - Anne Pierre

BABY DEDICATION

The first Sunday of each month has become an event at the church. This is perhaps due to the baby dedications that are conducted during this service. Each month, parents come and publicly present their child to the Lord, symbolically declaring to raise them in the way of the Lord.

This is a precious time for the parents and child; however, much work is conducted behind the scenes to ensure that this service is conducted smoothly.

1. First, parents must complete the Information for Baby Dedication Certificates form. Here is a copy of the form.

NEW LIFE
TABERNACLE
New Day, New Hope, New Purpose.

INFORMATION FOR
BABY DEDICATION CERTIFICATES

Please complete the following form. **PRINT IN ALL BLOCK CAPTIAL LETTERS**

Baby's Name _____
         First   Last

Day of Birth _____
        Month   Day   Year
Hospital _____

Mother's Name _____
         First   Last

Father's Name _____
         First   Last

If you would like to be added to our mailing list where you will receive information about upcoming events, please fill in your address and signature of authorization.

Address _____

City_____ State: _____ ZIP _____

Signature _____

FOR OFFICE USE ONLY:
Baby to be dedicated on: _____
             Date

SR. PASTOR DANIEL M. DAVY
PASTOR RASHIDI. F. COLLINS
6912 Williams Road PH (813) 740-1868
Seffner, FL 33584-2818 FAX (813) 612-5432
www.YourNLT.com
NewLife@YourNLT.com

2. Upon the completion of the form, our team contacts the parents to confirm the date of the dedication and verify the information provided.

3. Once contact has been made and the information verified, a Baby Dedication Certificate is printed.

Baby Dedication

This Certifies that

ANN CAMPBELL

Was dedicated to the Lord Jesus on

July 04, 2017 at

NEW LIFE TABERNACLE, UPC, INC.

Daniel M. Davy, Pastor   Date

NEW LIFE
TABERNACLE

4. In addition to the certificate, we print the Training Our Children booklet, which provides a wealth of information on raising children with Biblical support. This booklet, along with the certificate, complimentary photo of the child, and flowers are presented to the parents during the dedication.

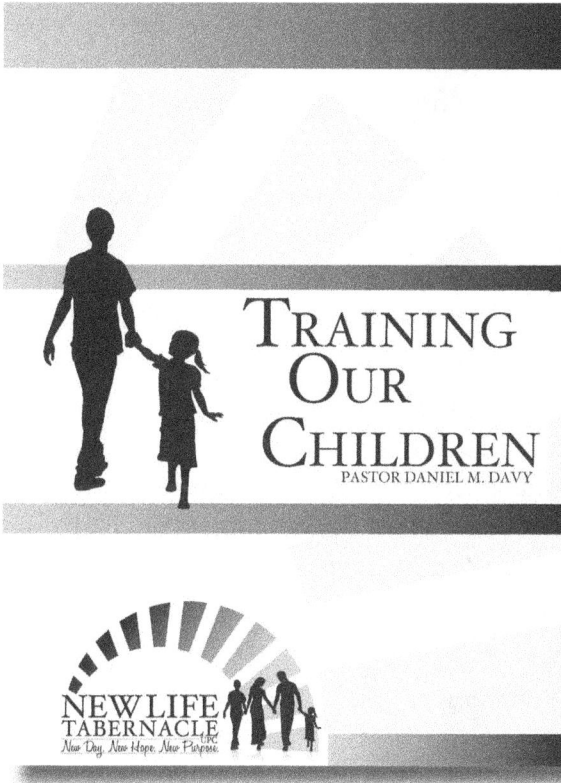

TRAINING
OUR
CHILDREN
PASTOR DANIEL M. DAVY

NEW LIFE
TABERNACLE UPC
New Day, New Hope, New Purpose.

During the initial call with the parent, we inform them of the pre-service photo shoot available to them. Our photographers come at early as 9:30am (30 minutes before Sunday School) to take photos of the precious jewels. A photo of each child is transferred to our Media team who displays the picture, along with the name of the child when the pastor calls the family up to the altar. This is perhaps one of the best moments during dedication as the audience reactions are priceless. As a parent, hearing the "Ooos' and Ahhh's" brings a smile to mine (and the guests) faces.

Special seating is assigned for the families. It is important to place them in the front rows of the church. Firstly, this ensures that they are attentive and engaged in the service.

Secondly, the likelihood of them leaving after the dedication is minimal. Note: baby dedication is a great outreach tool. Finally, it helps to orchestrate the service better and reduces the time, tremendously.

5. When the child is called up, a minister holds the child. We are grateful to have several ministers in our church, which means that each minister is assigned a child. The Pastor anoints the children with oil and the entire congregations pray over the children.

This event is near and dear to my heart. Remember, it was at a baby dedication service that I was able to hear the Gospel. I thank God that both members and non-members can experience Him and His salvation through this event. The church family puts their best foot forward to ensure that everything is done with the spirit of excellence.

HOSPITAL VISITATIONS

This should be a no-brainer, but I was shocked to discover that many churches no longer conduct hospital visitations. As I previously mentioned, people don't care how much you know until they know how much you care. Having to go to the hospital can be a scary and daunting experience. This is why having someone to visit and pray for him or her is important. As saints, we know that the prayers of the righteous availeth much. And we ought to apply our faith, even when the person in need lacks faith. In doing so, they will be reminded of the power of our God and their faith will, in most cases, not be waivered when crisis comes.

During hospital visits, God has used me time after time to reach others, even strangers. I can recall several times where after praying with someone at the hospital, people would come to me after hearing me pray, and ask me to pray for them. They would also request that I visit their loved ones and pray for them.

SPECIALS SERVICES

Our church has a dynamic Events Ministry; however, there are a few services, which the Guest Services coordinate. They are:

- Friends & Family Day
- Back to Church Sunday
- Honoring Our Veterans
- All Nations Sunday

Each service is designed to reach those who may not normally attend services. After each service a special reception is prepared just for our guests. Church members attend with the purpose of making our guests feel welcomed. I should note that these services are well attended, primarily due to communication sent via email and postal service in the weeks leading to the services. Also, the call team calls the guests encouraging them to attend. The outreach team is also helpful with promoting these services. This proves that when ministries work together, it produces the best results. Many of our guests and new converts also participate in these events. It's a great way of keeping them connected and involved.

THE YELLOW RIBBONS

I am always looking for ways to make our guests feel welcome. But what of the backsliders or those who are no longer attending the services? What do you do when you've called, visited, emailed, sent a letter or note… and nothing happens? At times, all we can do is…pray. That's right. Just because they no longer attend the church does not mean that we should not pray for them.

65

Lauren Wilkerson, a member of the church, sent me a message that was preached at a conference. This message was in line with our interaction with the souls we encounter, especially those who were no longer attend our services. What Lauren did not know was that I was reading a book at the time titled *Reharvested Fields: Back Sliders, The Heartbeat of God* by David S. McKemy, which confirmed a lot of the points in the message.

One of the things I continue to ask the Lord for is that He gives me His heart and teach me to love like He does. After listening to that message and hearing the story and the significance of the yellow ribbon, and how much it coincide with what I was reading, at the time, I knew the Lord wanted me to hear that message. I presented the idea with the team, and they too loved the idea.

I asked Lauren to purchase the yellow ribbon and had Kylia Campbell, another member of the church who so happen to be a seamstress, along with some of the ladies of the I AM Special mentorship group to assist with taping the ribbons on the trees located throughout the property. I wanted as many of the Greeters and those young ladies that assist us on Sunday to understand the reason why I greet the way I do.

It was important to ensure that the ribbons were placed where people would see them. As people enter the property, and drive down the driveway, or even from the highway - the ribbons are noticeable. The ribbons serve as a reminder to pray for the lost and backsliders for they are the heartbeat of God as seen in the following scriptures:

Jeremiah 3:14 Turn, O backsliding children, saith the LORD; for I am married unto you: and I will take you one of a city, and two of a family, and I will bring you to Zion:

Luke 15: 7 I say unto you, that likewise joy shall be in

heaven over one sinner that repenteth, more than over ninety and nine just persons, which need no repentance.

Giving the awesome opportunity that I have to work with members, guests, new converts and backsliders my prayer and expectation is that every time I stand in the foyer with the wonderful group of people in the ministry, someone is returning home today in Jesus' name. And God never failed us in this endeavor. When they walk through the doors of the church, our arms are open wide, and with a smile on our face, we show them, without words needed, they know that they are home; and we have been waiting for them!

Impact of the Ministry

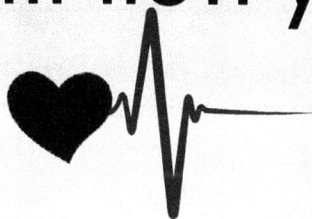

It is in our actions, dedication, and consistency that we are able to produce the results needed to really impact the overall mission of the church, seeking and saving that which is lost.

Oftentimes it is easy to feel that what you do in the ministry does not make a difference. You feel it's okay to miss church or leave the ministry altogether because you are not needed. When you find yourself feeling this way, you must cast down those strong imaginations, because they are the work of the enemy. Satan wants you to feel useless in the kingdom. He wants you to think that you don't matter when it comes to God's plans. This is far from the truth.

In this chapter, you will witness how the Guest and Usher ministry has made an impact on the lives of others in the House of God.

It was a turbulent time in my life. I was a 20-year-old wife and mother, and my husband was addicted to drugs, amongst other things. I first stepped into New Life Tabernacle on Easter Sunday, 2001 to simply meet up with my mother to commute for Easter dinner. A Brother, Courtney Campbell, ushered my then 3-month-old baby and me inside even though I wanted to wait outside until their service was complete. The altar call was so incredible I wanted to come back and visit for a full actual service. In that moment, I had no idea that I would never return to my old church again! Sister Ann Richardson (Campbell now), in the most sincere way, full of love and compassion, made that decision for me.

Living in hell at home, New Life Tabernacle became my only refuge and Sis Ann Campbell represented the love of the church I desperately needed. She made it her business to reach after my heart, and my soul, for God. There were times I was so overwhelmed with depression I would make excuses not to come to church, but she would never take no for an answer! One time I thought I would outsmart her by telling her my husband took the car, and that my baby and I would stay home because service had already started. Sis Ann instead outsmarted me by sending someone I would later know as Brother Ben to come pick us up, and we were never without a ride again. I was not use to all of this attention and someone caring about me.

A memory that goes beyond the boundaries of church sisterhood was when one day I was at work at CVS and my husband called with bad news that resulted in us having no money to pay bills. Ann walked into my job in the midst of all this and I briefly told her what happened because I was really busy. I think she asked me where my locker was or something, because she needed to borrow something, again I was busy so it's a blur. All I know is when my shift was over and I looked down in my purse, it was a significant amount of money in my purse from her.

I always tear up when someone asks about Ann Campbell because I can't find the right words to describe her. We share the same name, so I find it charming that she calls me "lil Sis' and I call her 'big Sis'. She is beyond a church sister or guest services leader, she's the genuine compassion and true representation of God's love of his people, to bring and keep us in His church. - Ann Johnson

My family and I moved to Florida from Brooklyn, NY in 2007. One of my concerns was finding an Apostolic church that really preached truth. We stayed with my aunt who lived right around corner from New Life on 109th. She knew we went to church and she saw I felt out of place on Sundays just sitting in her house. So I remember her saying to me "There

*is a Sunday church around the corner that my husband's
family visits when they come in town." She is Seventh Day
Adventist that's why she referred to it as a "Sunday" Church.
So I told her ok I will visit it on that coming Sunday. And I did.
My husband was still in NY at this time. So I took my three
girls and my cousin who was familiar with New Life.*

*I, of course, was nervous because I didn't know what to
expect and I needed my girls to be in church because that
was life for them. I was just praying that this would be our
place of worship. Plus the pressure was on me because my
husband was not with us for us to follow HIS lead instead of
mine. Well, when we walked through the doors I was greeted
by the greeters who were so nice and welcoming and it
made me feel at peace. I met Sis Ann and I filled out my
information. Her demeanor was so warm and loving. When
I gave her my contact information, I didn't expect it to go
anywhere. I just thought it was for records or whatever.*

*That Monday I was at my aunt's house and my aunt told
me someone was at the door for me. I was confused because
I was new to Florida so I wondered who on earth would be
visiting me? When I went to the door I saw it was Sis Ann
with a gift bag for me! I was so surprised and grateful that
she took the time out to come and visit me. After that first
meeting, it was history! I didn't just gain a friend I gained a
sister. We sat at my aunt's house for HOURS talking like we
were old friends catching up. Sis Ann has been more than
a blessing to my family and me. She has truly been a real
big sister to me. I can tell her any and everything and know
without a doubt she will take it to her grave.*

*After a while Sis Ann asked me if I wanted to join the
Greeters ministry. I remember telling her no because I am a
shy person and I can't see myself taking that initiative to just*

go up to someone and speak to them. But Sis Ann has a way of convincing you and so I gave it a try. Becoming a Greeter has certainly gotten me out of my "shy shell." It has helped me not only in church, but in my personal life as well. I can go up and speak to anyone now. I am extremely grateful at how God orchestrated this whole meeting with Sis Ann and the Greeters' ministry. I love her and the burden she has for this ministry. And this encounter with her let me know without a shadow of doubt, that God definitely makes no mistakes!
- Kerry Browne

Being able to serve as a greeter at New Life Tabernacle is an amazing, life changing experience and is also quite humbling. The best part about greeting is Morning Prayer. Words can hardly describe what it is like to be praying for those that God is sending each Sunday morning before they get to church. When we pray my focus shifts to those coming in, and off myself or any other thing that could be a distraction. No matter what is going on, we lay it down before the Lord in prayer and shift our focus to the needs of those who are on their way. I don't worry about my clothes, my hair or my shoes after that! As believers we know the Lord is with us at all times but Sunday morning prayer really reminds me that we're here to do the will of God and that He is with us as each one of us do His work. When we bond together in prayer on those Sunday mornings the presence of God is so awesome, it's hard to put any of it into words. I've never had this experience anywhere else before, and to see a leader, Sis Ann Campbell, not just give us direction but also be a vivid example for us to follow motivates me to keep working. I take note of how she greets the guests as they come in and how those that are returning are delighted to see her. As they approach, she meets them with a smile and a hug. She is one of the warmest, most loving persons I know and she's genuine about it!! She never gets tired of encouraging us and showing how much she appreciates what we do, knowing it's all to the glory of our Lord Jesus Christ. As we greet, she reminds us to pray as we look out because God is sending the people. What an amazing way to help us catch the vision! I remember thinking to myself one day about how Sis Ann always says "love you sis" and realizing that she really means it when she says it. It makes all the difference. I'm amazed at what the Lord is doing through her and through this ministry! It's an honor to be a doorkeeper in the house of God! I love you Sis Ann!!! May the Lord continue to bless you and your family! - Daniella Gordan

I am always grateful to God, for having someone like Sister Ann Campbell in my life. When I moved to Tampa 3 years ago, New Life Tabernacle was one of the churches I considered visiting. A family member insisted that I find and stick to Sis Ann Campbell because "she is as sweet as punch". So I must say that her honorable reputation precedes her. Ann has always treated me like her own daughter and my children like her own. In times where I didn't have any money or food, Ann always looked out for us.

Ann is ALWAYS pouring into the lives of others, and I admire how she can remember EVERY visitor's name that steps in the doors of New Life Tabernacle. God has constantly given Ann divine opportunities to reach out to people and compel them to give their lives to Jesus. I have watched this woman travail in prayer over the burden that she carries for lost souls, even to the point of pure exhaustion. For those of us who have the spiritual gift of serving and helps, Sis Ann Campbell consistently trains us in excellence and love through Guest Services and Benevolence Ministry. She is very sensitive to the needs of others and puts their needs above her own. Ann is truly a blessing to all who come into contact with her, and I love her dearly. - Candace Edwards

My experience as a greeter is like planting a seed of kindness with every smile, hug, compassion, or helpfulness shown to members and visitors. Humans naturally have a desire to be accepted and welcomed where ever we may go; whether it is a new church, a local restaurant, or Wal-Mart. Feeling welcomed is a major part of any new personal experience. Greeting is such an honor, as you are the first person to interact with people as they come to find a place of worship, renew faith, build relationships, or find hope. Greeting allows you to get to know people who come from different backgrounds. You are able to influence people in positive ways. It is an opportunity to show compassion or simply add a spurt of light into someone else's life. Something as simple as remembering someone's name can make them feel like part of the family. Greeting opens doors to connect and build relationships. We are representatives of Christ as we stand at the doors. Jesus' mission is to seek and save the lost. We must show the genuine love of Christ to fulfill his mission. As greeters, we anticipate the needs of others, whether is a spiritual need for encouragement and direction, or a physical need. It's exciting to hear reports of the warmth a guest may have felt while visiting New Life or accounts of walking through the doors and knowing "this is home". This is exactly where they should be, and I believe greeting is a difference maker! - Jaleesa Murphy

I have known Ann Campbell for quite some time even before New Life and I believe it is by God's design he has reconnected us. Ann is much more than a friend, she is my big sister and mentor who leads with passion and by example. As a greeter when God lead her to ask me about greeting I didn't think I would be a good candidate. But as I prayed and asked God to direct me He lead me to say yes. Being a person who is laid back, it takes me a while to warm up to people so I knew it would be a challenge for me. However, I had the opportunity to attend a training Ann did at another church and as she taught, and went through the greeters role and different steps from the parking lot to the baptismal to following up and being in constant contact with a new convert I was amazed. Being in this ministry helps in their growing, and it takes the entire body of Christ to assist. As I watched her in awe that day, there was an awaking in me as if she told me a prized secret. From that day forward, I begin to realize my own passion. I have always loved people and cared strongly for their well being, and as Ann pours into me she is dragging out of me that same passion she has which I now understand is a gifting from God. As a big sister, wow I can go on and on but I am so grateful God has blessed me with Ann. There is not a time I cannot call her or text and she is not there. Whether shopping or just talking on the phone her encouragement is always present. The love and passion within her is too vast for her earthly vessel to hold and God is directing her to those in whom she can pour her overflow into. I count it a privilege I have been included to partake in it and I am forever grateful and thankful.
- Claytimis T. Osagie

What it means to be a greeter. Being a greeter means a lot more than opening a door and welcoming people into the house of God. It starts by being focused in prayer, and focused enough to become sensitive to those entering into the gates. Understanding, feeling, and relating to those coming in trodden, hurt, and despondent, can be the difference that it takes to ushering in the presence of the Lord, not only to the congregation but to that person particularly. Over the years that I have greeted at New Life Tabernacle I have come to know those who have come and gone, and those who are still here with us. Not only by first name, but also on a first, last, and entire family basis. I've seen people grow old, as they have seen me grow old. Not in the physical sense, but grow older in the Lord, growing to understand that it means more than just standing at the door in matching outfits, it is being a doorkeeper in the house of the Lord. There is a very distinct difference, understood by those who have been a part of the ministry. I cherish the experiences that we have had as a group and that I have had personally at the door. There have been times where each of us, I'm sure, have wanted to give up the position, but when we look back and realize why it is that we have been placed within this ministry, we understand that it's not about us at all, but that it's ALL about Jesus! - Diane Williams

I have usually been a shy and reserved person. That's kind of how I wanted to stay too.... to myself. However, the moment I met Ann Campbell, she had other plans for my shyness!

I was asked to join the Greeters' team shortly after meeting Sis Ann. She said... "There is something about you that I like, and I want you to join Guest Services!" I was reluctant at first, but Sis Ann was so genuine in the way that she said it... so I said OK!!

Shortly after serving in the Guest Services Ministry, I was pushed and pulled in all kinds of directions; spiritually and physically, and mentally. I was forced to serve others outside of my comfort zone. I had to speak to people I've never met before, I had to make conversation... and be genuine about it, and I had to learn a good lesson in humility.

Throughout all of the changes that were happening to me in serving in the Guest Services Ministry, I can never say that it got too hard to do. Sis Ann was ALWAYS there to direct me, correct me, and encourage me. She knew JUST what to say to me, and when to say it. I looked up to her because I saw how important it was to serve others in this ministry. Sis Ann taught me to see that I wasn't just greeting people at a door... Sis Ann taught me that I was making a difference in people's lives by simply connecting with them and showing them how much we care about them.

So here I am now, 5 years later... no longer shy; no longer timid; no longer selfish. My personal and spiritual life has flourished under Sis Ann's guidance. She became a second mother to me. My prayer life has also developed because she showed me how important it was to pray for others. My personal life has developed because she showed me that some of the best friendships come from just being genuine with people and connecting on a personal level.

If I had never met Sis Ann, I don't know if I would be the person that I am today. I love my new personality; I love my church family more than anything; I love meeting new people all the time... and it would have never been this way if I didn't trust what Ann Campbell saw in me the first time she met me.

I'm so grateful to have Sis Ann in my life. I thank God for orchestrating it. - Angelina Colhouer

I've always had this bad habit of not really sharing my life issues with too many people. There are times when I can be extremely ill and no one will ever know it. I'm getting better, but it's just not something I ever really did in the past. I remember when I was hospitalized in 2014, due to severe migraines. It was the first time my condition was actually diagnosed. I went through a three or four-day hospital stay and it was intense! I had to have a spinal tap procedure and they wanted to make sure my spinal fluid levels had balanced before sending me home. I think maybe one or two people from the church knew about it, because I told them. The others knew something was wrong because I had asked for prayers on my Facebook page.

Some way or another, Sister Ann found out about it and it became apparent to me once I returned to church that following Sunday. She walked up to me and smiled and gave me the biggest hug. Then she let me have it! LOL. She is such a big sister to EVERY ONE! To know her is to love her. She told me I better not ever go to the hospital again and not let her know about it. I told her okay and she asked if I needed anything. She said if I needed any cleaning or cooking done, to let her know and she will have her team over to take care of me.

A few months later, I was in the hospital again for the same issue. I forgot to call Sis. Ann! Of course, once again, she found out I was in the hospital and as soon as I saw her face when I returned to service, it dawned on me that I had made that same mistake twice. This time she pleaded with me. She said, "Sis you have to let me know when you are in the hospital or sick or even lose a loved one. This is what I am here for. This entire ministry is because of situations like this. I have an entire team dedicated to take care of you and your loved ones when things like this happen. If this happens *again, please let me know." I told her okay and that day I vowed to always let her know if something was going on with me. There was such a genuine concern from her and I knew she truly meant every word she'd said.*

So in January of 2016, when I loss a pregnancy and was hospitalized because of it, I made sure I let her know. Sure enough, I saw Sis Ann in action. Once I made it home from the hospital, she called me and said she and another member of the team was on their way to me. She asked if I was hungry and she said she would stop by Publix and get what I needed. When they got to my house, she asked if I needed anything (like cooking, cleaning, taking care of the kids), I told her no because my husband was going to be home with me for a week and by then I should have my strength back. She stayed with me for about thirty minutes and talked and ministered to me. I was a bit down because of the loss of my baby and she let me know that she would be there if I needed her. THAT SPOKE VOLUMES! Before leaving that day, she and her team member prayed my husband and me and she told me to call her if I needed anything. I didn't call, but just knowing I had the option made a world of difference.

I will never forget all the times Sis. Ann, and the ministries she oversees, has blessed my life. She is truly a Godsend. I love her dearly and I thank God for her genuine and loving spirit. I know that her ministry will continue to be blessed because she is truly a follower after God's own heart. Thank you, for everything, Sis. Ann! - Arlisha Myrie

You may be in a tough time, but the enemy always fights you the hardest when he knows God has something great in store for you.

The statement has been said you should know 69 people in church by their name. I took the challenge on by joining the

Guest Services Ministry in which I was able to learn people and their names. Little did I know, God had prepared me at a young age to work with this ministry even before coming to Tampa.

My journey began when Sis Ann Campbell took me under her wing and showed me her love , compassion, and dedication to this ministry. I can remember countless times going places and seeing the people in their homes, completing hospital visits, or simply being in the store and always hearing Sis Ann say, "Shannon, do you have church cards with you?", Taking that time with her has allowed me to show that same affection to others and see them come to church because someone took that same time to care for me
- Shannon Simon

I will never forget the Sunday morning when Ann approached me and suggested that I should consider greeting. I told her that it was amazing because I was considering to become a Greeter. This was many, many, many years ago and I have been greeting since that day. I am Thankful for Ann's sensitivity to the Lord's leading.

My life has been greatly impacted since being under the Leadership of Ann Campbell. She has challenged, encouraged, corrected, cared for, and most of all genuinely loved me.

I love the unity that has been cultivated among the greeters. I always look forward to our greeters' prayer time every Sunday morning at 9:30 a.m. I am very good with smiling through difficult times. But Ann always seems to sense when I am not okay. She has prayed with me and cried with me and for that I am forever grateful. God has truly used her to bless my life and I love and appreciate her so very much.
- Temika Coker

Knowing and understanding your purpose is one of the most fulfilling gifts God will ever give you. Many people may feel like me, wondering why on earth the Pastor would expect me to go be a greeter when it was only a one-time deal. Or you may feel like Kerry and think you are far too shy to do something that requires you to see everyone that comes through the door. Perhaps you may even be ready and willing to jump into whatever purpose God has planned in your life. One thing's for certain, you always want to position yourself in such a way that you can be used by God. In my situation, I had to check my attitude and make sure I was not hindering the work of God when my Pastor saw something in me that I didn't. In Kerry, she had to change her focus and not dwell so much on her fear, but focus more on her trust in knowing that the person that approached her may have been sent by God to do so. And lastly, you, you may be in a place where you are wondering what your purpose is. I implore you to have an open mind and heart. Truly seek after God and know that it is through Him and Him alone that you can do anything. Selah

www.ingramcontent.com/pod-product-compliance
Lightning Source LLC
Chambersburg PA
CBHW071421040426
42445CB00012BA/1238